Life on
MARS

David Getz

illustrated by Peter McCarty

Revised Edition

Henry Holt and Company ✦ New York

For Jacqui, to whom I will always go when Phobos and Deimos
circle overhead, and for Maxine, our captain aboard this ship.
Where will you take us? And much thanks to my mom, Dr. Amato,
JoAnn, Cathy, Dr. Bierman, the Ronald McDonald House, the Clown
Care Unit, everybody at Schneider Children's Hospital, and that
woman who made us buy the fluffy snowman. Hello, Simi!

Acknowledgments
Thanks to the following people for the time in personal interviews
they gave me: Louis Friedman, president of the Planetary Society; Chris McKay
of NASA, Ames Research Center; Tom Meyer, Boulder Center for Science
and Policy; Dr. Arnauld Nicogossian, chief medical officer of NASA;
Robert Zubrin of Martin Marietta; Nadine Barlow, director of the University
of Central Florida Robinson Observatory; and the astronauts: Leroy Chiao,
Ph.D., Marsha Ivins; and Colonel Steve Nagel, USAF

Henry Holt and Company, LLC / *Publishers since 1866*
115 West 18th Street / New York, New York 10011
www.henryholt.com

Henry Holt is a registered trademark of Henry Holt and Company, LLC
Text copyright © 1997 by David Getz / Illustrations copyright © 1997 by Peter McCarty
All rights reserved. Distributed in Canada by H. B. Fenn and Company Ltd.

Library of Congress Cataloging-in-Publication Data
Getz, David. Life on Mars / by David Getz.
p.   cm.
Summary: Presents information about Mars as the reader joins a hypothetical
three-year space exploration of the planet costing fifty billion dollars and requiring
fifty-four thousand pounds of food, water, and oxygen.
ISBN-13: 978-0-8050-7729-2
ISBN-10: 0-8050-7729-4
1. Life on other planets—Juvenile literature.   2. Mars (Planet)—Juvenile literature.
[1. Life on other planets. 2. Mars (Planet).]   I. Title.
QB54.G48 1995   574.999'23—dc20   95-20504
First published as a Redfeather Book in 1997
Revised edition—2004
Printed in the United States of America on acid-free paper. ∞
1   3   5   7   9   10   8   6   4   2

Contents

Life on MARS

Within minutes your ship will leave its Earth orbit.

Blast-off

Your commander turns down the lights in the cabin to cut the glare. It is night and you are flying southeast, across the United States. You are in your last orbit, a few hundred miles up. You can identify all of the major cities by their lights. You pass over the Gulf of Mexico and down across South America. And then, as the lights of Buenos Aires fade from view, you see a shooting star slash a white stripe through the atmosphere beneath you.

You are looking down at shooting stars. How wonderful.

"Get ready to say good-bye," your commander says.

Within minutes your ship will leave its Earth orbit.

You are going to Mars. You will be the first humans to visit another planet.

The sun begins to rise over Earth's horizon. You glance back down at your home. You will not see your family again for almost three years.

You are high enough to see the curvature of Earth. You stare at the fluorescent blue band on the horizon. It is the Earth's atmosphere, the layer of air that surrounds the planet. You are struck by how thin the atmosphere looks on the horizon. How strange it is to be looking down on the air that fills the lungs of 4 billion people.

Where you are going, there will be no air to fill your lungs. Mars's atmosphere is one hundred times thinner than Earth's. It is too thin to breathe. It lacks oxygen. It is almost entirely carbon dioxide, the same stuff that makes up the bubbles in your soft drink.

You steal another glance at Earth. It is mostly white and blue. White from drifting clouds, blue from the oceans.

Clouds will be a rare sight on Mars. You will never see an ocean. There are no oceans on Mars, no rivers, streams, lakes, or ponds. No puddles. Mars is bone-dry. There is no flowing water anywhere on its surface.

No air to breathe, no water to drink.

"Ready to fire rockets," your commander announces.

Your commander's timing must be perfect. The Earth races around the sun at over 70,000 miles per hour! As you orbit 250 miles above the ground, gravity keeps you connected to this speeding Earth, as if by a long string. When your commander fires the rockets, that "string" will be severed, and your ship will be flung away from Earth at 70,000 miles per hour, plus the speed your rockets have given you. The sun's gravity will slow you down a little and set you on a curving path that will eventually intersect the path Mars takes as it orbits the sun.

This slide from one racing planet to another is called the *Hohman transfer*. The trip from the Earth to Mars is a long one, over 250 million miles, and it takes 6 months.

And then there's the stay.

Since the planets orbit the sun at different speeds and at different distances, you cannot "leap" from

Earth to Mars at any time. Leaving too soon or too late will cause you to miss Mars altogether. Make a mistake, and you will wind up just another dark object forever orbiting the sun. Your *launch window*, the moment when it is possible to be flung from the Earth to Mars, occurs about once every two years and lasts only a few weeks. Similarly, you will have to wait eighteen months on Mars before it is safe to be flung back home.

Six months to get there; a year-and-a-half stay; six months to get back.

"Firing the rockets," your commander announces.

You hope your five crewmates are good company.

You watch your home planet recede.

You remove from your pocket one of the funny postcards your parents brought you from the Planetary Society.

"Vacationing on Mars," it says. "Wish you were here."

The card shows a photo of Mars taken from the unmanned *Viking* spacecraft that landed on the planet in 1976. It reveals a dramatic desert landscape complete with sand dunes and huge boulders. Though the ground is pink, it does not appear much different from the deserts of southern Colorado or Nevada. The scientist Carl Sagan once said he would not have been too surprised to see a prospector and a mule appear in one of these photos.

Except this mule and the prospector would have to be wearing space suits.

You turn the card over. You will not see your family again for almost three years.

Why are you going?

Facts About Mars

- Diameter (distance around equator): 4,199 miles (0.53 times Earth's)
- Rotation (length of Martian day): 1.03 Earth days
- Revolution (time it takes to travel around the sun): 686.9 Earth days
- Distance from sun: 141 million miles
- Moons: Phobos and Deimos
- Temperature: 50° F day; – 148° F night
- Surface gravity: 0.38 times Earth's
- Atmosphere: mostly carbon dioxide; one hundredth as dense as Earth's

---

(*From* Ad Astra's Traveller's Guide to Mars)

Martians in Our Mirrors

You are going to find out about life on Mars.

Is there life on Mars?

Mars is a small planet that is very far away. At its closest, Mars is 35 million miles from Earth. In the night sky, Mars appears small enough to fit into one of the moon's craters.

Without a powerful telescope, it is impossible to see any detail of the surface of the planet.

But that has not stopped people from seeing what they wanted. And for thousands of years, people saw life.

In 1749, Benjamin Franklin wrote that all the important philosophers and mathematicians of his time thought the planets supported life.

Some people on Earth expressed a burning desire to communicate with the inhabitants of Mars.

In 1819, Johann von Littrow, the director of the observatory at Vienna, Austria, proposed attracting the Martians' attention by lighting huge fires on Earth in the shape of geometric patterns.

In the 1870s, Charles Cros, of France, suggested writing directly on the surface of Mars. His idea was to tilt an immense magnifying glass in such a way that it would burn letters onto the Martian desert.

Though neither proposal was carried out, many scientists nevertheless were sure there was life on Mars. On December 17, 1900, the Guzman Prize committee of France announced an award: One hundred thousand francs would go to the first person to make contact with intelligent beings on another planet. Since the committee members were already convinced there was life on Mars, communicating with a Martian wouldn't win you the prize. It was considered too easy.

In 1894, the American astronomer Percival Lowell built an observatory in Flagstaff, Arizona, solely to study Mars. Looking through his powerful telescope,

Lowell observed straight lines on the planet's surface. He believed the lines were canals built to carry water from the polar ice caps to the inhabitants of dry cities on the Martian equator. Lowell concluded that Mars was an old planet, running out of water, populated with intelligent, engineering-minded creatures.

No other observer of Mars saw the lines Lowell had seen. No scientist could reproduce his findings. Something was wrong with either Lowell's telescope or with Lowell himself. Perhaps it was his eyes, or perhaps he was simply seeing what he wanted to see.

Though few scientists took him seriously, Lowell convinced many people that there was life on Mars. Clearly, many people wanted there to be life on Mars. Lowell said what they wanted to hear. Science-fiction writers adapted Lowell's ideas to create countless books about Martians.

In 1922, and again in 1924, when Mars was as close as it gets to Earth, the U.S. government asked all radio stations to remain quiet so it could listen for Martian broadcasts.

Operators were standing by. . . .

The War of the Worlds *convinced many listeners that Martians had invaded Earth.*

No Martian calls were received.

Then, in 1938, on the night before Halloween, Martians invaded New Jersey.

At least that's what the man on the radio announced. Blasting heat-ray guns and spraying poisonous gas, the Martian army destroyed anyone who stood in its path. American troops were helpless.

Listening to the radio reports, one woman grabbed her son, sat down, and wept.

Thousands of listeners called their police stations. Some wanted to know where they could hide. Others volunteered their help.

In New Jersey, one man bravely decided to take on the Martians single-handed. Leveling his gun, he took aim and shot at an approaching spaceship. Only it wasn't an approaching spaceship; it was a water tower.

The Martians were not invading. It was just a radio play based on H. G. Wells's book *The War of the Worlds*.

Clearly, Mars has stimulated our imaginations. Many creative writers have populated Mars with a wonderful variety of good and evil beings. Millions of people have read these books and have believed, at least for a moment, that what they read was true. We have been like children alone in our rooms, eagerly

convincing ourselves there are monsters in our closets.
   Then again, maybe we weren't so wrong.
   There now is evidence of intelligent life on Mars.
   Except it is ours.

3

Hello? Hello? Anybody Home?

Early in the morning of July 20, 1976, scientists at the Jet Propulsion Laboratory in Pasadena, California, sent a radio message to the *Viking 1* probe orbiting Mars.

"Release lander!"

Mars was on the other side of the sun from Earth, 200 million miles away. At light speed, the message traveled for 19 minutes before it reached the *Viking* craft. *Viking 1* did as it was told. It released its 1,300-pound lander. One half of the most expensive biology experiment in history began to fall through the pink Martian sky.

In a period of over eight years, ten thousand people

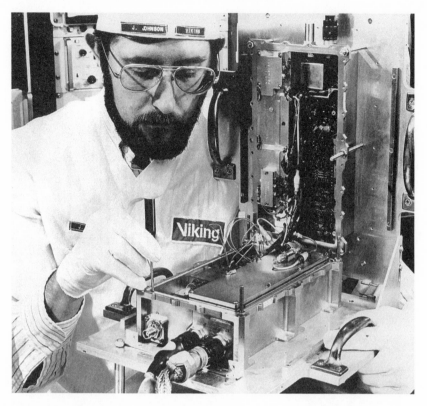

A UHF radio that was part of the first broadcasting station on Mars.
(NASA)

had helped design and build two *Viking* spacecraft that would answer the question "Is there life on Mars?"

The project cost 1 billion dollars. Each *Viking* consisted of an orbiter and a lander. Both craft were launched from Cape Canaveral, Florida, in the

A Viking *orbiter floats above the Martian horizon.*

summer of 1975: *Viking 1* on August 20, *Viking 2* on
September 9.

Viking 1's lander used its heat shield, parachute,
and rockets to ease its descent through the thin

Martian atmosphere. If the lander had settled on a boulder, or even a large rock, it could have tipped over and broken.

Three hours and thirteen minutes after it began its fall from the sky, the *Viking* lander touched down

A *full-scale model of the* Viking *spaceship* (NASA)

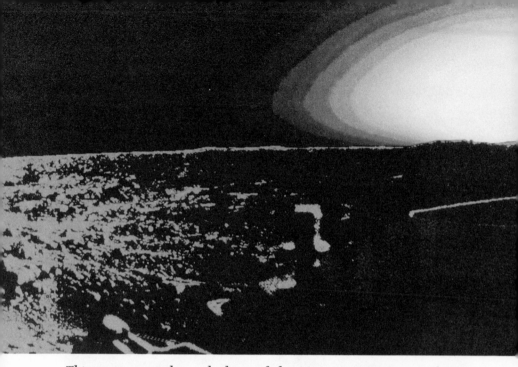

This computer-enhanced photo of the Martian sunset over Chryse Planitia *was taken by* Viking 1 *on August 20, 1976.* (NASA)

safely on the western slope of *Chryse Planitia* (the "Plains of Gold").

It radioed home. Nineteen minutes later, mission control announced, "Touchdown!"

Everyone leapt and shouted for joy. It was four A.M.

Two months later, on September 3, the lander from *Viking 2* also settled down safely on the treacherous Martian terrain.

How would the landers determine if anybody was home?

Five feet above the ground, or the height of a short thirteen-year-old, were the *Viking*'s "eyes." These two cameras searched not only for some lurking Martian beast or mini-beast, but for any changes in color or shape in the nearby scenery that could be caused by some form of life.

As a pit viper can detect the body heat given off by a mouse, the *Viking* landers used sensors to detect anything in the area that was radiating body heat.

Another sensor searched for anything giving off moisture. We give off moisture when we sweat or breathe.

Also equipped with *seismometers,* to detect quakes and tremors, the landers would have detected the heavy steps of any lumbering Martian creature.

Devices called *entry-mass spectronometers* analyzed the Martian air to determine if there were any gases that could come only from something living, as oxygen on Earth is let off by plants.

All was quiet. Nothing moved mysteriously, or

Viking 1 *digs a deep trench to obtain samples from the soil below the surface.* (NASA)

suspiciously changed its color. The *Vikings* failed to hear any footsteps or discover any warm bodies. There was no scent of life in the air.

But scientists didn't really expect there to be life *above* the Martian soil. The thin Martian atmosphere would make it impossible for any form of Earth life to survive aboveground. Animals couldn't breathe there. On Earth, we live at the bottom of our *atmosphere.* Just as water presses on a fish at all points of the fish's body, our atmosphere surrounds us and presses against us. To inhale, we expand our chests to allow this air to rush into our lungs. Since air contains oxygen, we can breathe.

On Mars the atmosphere is so thin, nothing would rush into our mouths. Even if you could take a deep breath, it would not do you much good. There is no oxygen in the Martian air.

And there is nothing to drink. The weight of Earth's atmosphere presses down on the planet's surface with about 16 pounds of force per square inch. A thinner atmosphere presses down on things with less force. It has less *air pressure.* When air pressure gets too low, liquid water evaporates. It instantly turns into water vapor. Liquid water cannot exist on the Martian surface.

And it is too cold, much colder than anyplace on Earth. The nearer a planet is to the sun, the more energy it receives to warm its surface during the day. A thick atmosphere acts as a blanket to trap that heat so it does not escape at night. Since Mars is much farther from the sun than Earth, and its atmosphere is much thinner, it is cold during the day and frighteningly cold at night. Temperatures at its *equator* can dip to a horrifying 150 degrees below zero.

And the Martian surface is bombarded with deadly ultraviolet radiation. Earth is surrounded by an ozone layer in the atmosphere, which shields us from most of the sun's ultraviolet radiation. Mars has no ozone layer at all.

But what about beneath the ground? Could some microscopic creature find moisture and protection in the pink Martian soil?

The *Viking* landers removed their shovels and began to dig.

A Very Expensive Bowl
of Chicken Soup

How do you look for life in a spoonful of dirt on another planet?

On Earth, the soil it would take to cover a penny contains anywhere from 100 million to 1 billion microscopic one-celled creatures called *microbes*.

Finding just one cell in the soil of Mars would have been a breathtaking discovery.

It seemed possible. Microbes can be pretty hardy. Recently, scientists drilling deep into Earth, where the temperatures reach 167 degrees Fahrenheit, found about a hundred different types of microbes. One such bug, *Bacillus infernus* ("bacillus from hell"), can live only where there is *no* oxygen.

Taking soil samples from Mars (NASA)

On the more frigid side, scientists have discovered lichen and bacteria growing inside rocks found in the dry valleys of Antarctica.

The *Vikings* brought three biology experiments designed to search for evidence of microbial life.

In the gas-exchange, or "chicken soup," experiment, the *Viking* landers "fed" to a sample of Martian soil a "soup" filled with nutritious chemicals. Scientists hoped that if something was alive in the soil, it would slurp up some of this broth, digest it, and give off telltale gases that indicated it was alive.

In a second experiment, the soil was again "fed," this time with radioactive food. If an organism ate this food, the *Viking* landers would be able to trace the radioactively tagged chemicals to see how they were consumed and changed by the living organism.

In both of these experiments, the landers added liquid water and water vapor to the Martian soil to make things more Earth-like.

In the third experiment, the landers tried to feed and incubate life in the Martian soil under Martian conditions. No water was added. The soil was then analyzed to look for any signs of life.

No gases were exchanged, no food digested, nothing grew, nothing breathed, nothing multiplied. All three experiments failed to detect any signs of Martian life.

But did that mean nothing had ever lived on Mars, or nothing could live on Mars? Just as you might search a kitchen for flour and eggs and milk to see if you could make a cake, the *Vikings* searched the Martian soil for the ingredients of life.

On Earth, the simplest form of life is the cell. Cells are tiny. About a hundred of them could fit onto the period at the end of this sentence. Yet each cell carries on the basic functions of life. It eats, breathes, gives off wastes, reproduces, and dies.

The basic ingredient of cells is *protein*. There are thousands and thousands of different types of proteins. This variety of proteins is responsible for the variety of life. Proteins make a nerve cell different from a muscle cell, an amoeba different from a hydra.

But what are proteins made of? What makes one protein different from another? All proteins are made up of molecules called *amino acids*. There are only twenty types of amino acids. Just as the twenty-six letters of the English alphabet can combine to form all of the words in a dictionary, amino acids combine in various ways to form all of the proteins that make up life on Earth.

Amino acids are the basic units of life. And that is what the *Viking* landers looked for first in the Martian soil.

Both *Vikings* contained *gas chromatography mass spectrometers (GCMS)* that could detect the presence of one amino acid in 1 billion microscopic parts of Martian soil. They did not find any.

What is more, the *Vikings* discovered that the Martian soil is actually toxic. It seems that the ultraviolet radiation that bombards Mars reacts with the excessively dry soil to make it *antiseptic.* Martian soil actually destroys amino acids.

"The facts in the case," Dr. Chris McKay, a planetary scientist at NASA, says, "are that we look at Mars today and it looks as dead as a doornail."

The reason, McKay adds, is that Mars is dry.

"The one absolute requirement for life, for all organisms on Earth, is liquid water," Dr. McKay explains. "Everything else is negotiable. You have organisms for example that like oxygen, some that hate it. Some that like carbon dioxide, some that prefer methane. Some that like sulfur, some that don't. But the one absolute requirement for all life on Earth is liquid water."

But once upon a time, there was water on Mars.

This Old House

As your rocket ship quickly speeds away from Earth, you glance at another postcard from Mars.

The card shows the great canyon *Valles Marineris,* a series of gashes that cuts three miles deep into the Martian crust and spreads out across nearly 2,800 miles, the distance from New York to California.

You have seen other photos of Mars that show less dramatic scars in the Martian terrain—what appear to be empty riverbeds, hundreds of miles long, cut through the heavily cratered plains of Mars. How were these canyons and riverbeds formed? What tool carved up the Martian landscape?

At present, scientists can offer only this explanation:

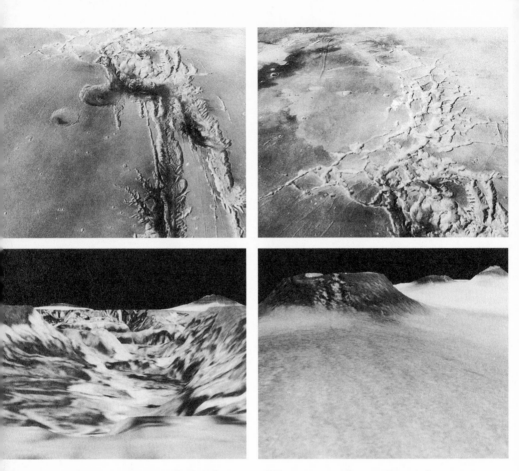

Four computer-enhanced views of the crevices that make up the great canyon Valles Marineris (NASA)

Facing page: *A network of channels on Mars that appear to have been made when large amounts of water came up from underground* (NASA)

It was water. Long ago, water rushed upward from beneath the Martian crust, causing the chaotic scarring of *Valles Marineris*. Rivers ran across the face of Mars.

If Mars had rivers, then it must have had a thicker, heavier atmosphere that prevented water from evaporating. A thicker, heavier atmosphere also traps more daytime heat. Mars was warmer. Of course! If Mars had flowing rivers, then the temperature must have been above freezing.

So once upon a time, it seems, Mars was warm. It had a thick atmosphere. Water moved along its surface. Mars, named after the Roman god of war, must have been a less hostile place to visit. Perhaps it was even pleasant enough for some form of life to call it home.

But when was this "once upon a time"?

To learn when the waters flowed, scientists counted the craters surrounding the rivers. Craters are holes caused by the impact of meteors. Planets accumulate craters with age. The more craters an area has, the older it is.

The Earth hides most of its meteor craters under its

Olympus Mons *is believed to be the largest volcano in the solar system.* (NASA)

oceans. Geologic activity, weather and water erosion, and plant life have erased or disguised most impacts on land. So it's not easy to count craters on Earth. But it is on Mars.

And scientists, studying photographs taken by

probes, counted many. The riverbeds on Mars are sat-
urated with craters. There are so many craters that scientists date the landscape back to the time when the
planets were still being formed. At that time the solar
system was filled with rocky debris. Meteors rained
down like hail. Appropriately, this period, about 3.8
billion years ago, is called the Great Bombardment.
What was Mars like during this period so long ago?

When a planet forms, a tremendous amount of heat
is trapped beneath its surface. This heat explodes
through the planet's crust in volcanic eruptions. Volcanoes also spew vast amounts of carbon dioxide and
water vapor into the air. This *outgassing* creates a
planet's atmosphere. It made the Martian air dense
and heavy with carbon dioxide.

Carbon dioxide is a *greenhouse gas*. It acts like the
windows of a greenhouse to retain heat. Most of the
sun's energy travels to a planet's surface as visible light.
The planet absorbs this energy, changes it into heat,
and then re-emits it as *infrared radiation*, which is
energy invisible to our eyes. Carbon dioxide traps
infrared radiation and prevents it from escaping into
space.

During the formation of Mars, volcanoes spewed large amounts of carbon dioxide and water vapor into the air, creating the planet's atmosphere.

So 3.8 billion years ago, Mars was warm. But was it livable?

Earth provides a clue.

Our home planet also possessed a thick carbon-dioxide atmosphere 3.8 billion years ago. There was no oxygen in the air. There was no ozone layer. Deadly ultraviolet radiation streamed down onto our planet's surface. Volcanoes continuously erupted. Water flowed over much of the surface.

And life on Earth thrived. In Shark's Bay, Australia, there are basketball-sized fossils of clusters of microscopic blue-green algae that lived 3.5 billion years ago.

When Mars and Earth had similar environments, Earth was populated. What about Mars?

Does life originate whenever the conditions are right? If it does, then life should have appeared on Mars.

If there was life on Mars, how different was it from life on Earth? And what happened to it? Could it be there still?

"About five years ago," Dr. McKay says, "we were sort of hit in the head when the Russians started telling us about organisms that they were finding in permafrost that had been frozen for three million years and were still alive. Thaw them out and they grow."

The *Viking* shovels only scraped the skin of the

planet. One inch deeper and ultraviolet radiation is harmless. Could something be sleeping beneath the Martian soil?

Was there life on Mars?

That is it. That is one half of the great mystery, one half of the reason why you are going to Mars.

Will there be life on Mars?

That's the other half.

6

I'll Huff and
I'll Puff and I'll . . .

Dr. Chris McKay sees Mars as a once-attractive home that collapsed. The Martian interior slowly cooled. Its volcanoes became inactive. Most of the carbon dioxide that remained in the atmosphere fell out of the sky into the soil to form carbonate rocks. The air thinned. Air pressure diminished. Some water evaporated and was lost into space. Some of the water became ice and combined with frozen carbon dioxide to form the Martian polar caps.

What happened to the rest?

"We think the water's frozen into the ground as permafrost," Dr. McKay states. Much of the surface of Mars resembles an old road with cracks, bulges, and potholes. Tom Meyers, an expert on Mars from the

University of Colorado, thinks this buckling could have been caused by underground water melting and then freezing again.

Peter Camerole, a planetary geologist for NASA, believes that the Martian crust is porous, or full of holes, to a depth of 10 miles. If that proves true, Camerole suggests the cold Martian crust could act like a sponge, trapping a frozen underground ocean that is a half mile deep.

As the rivers disappeared, Mars became what it is today, a cold, dry, lifeless planet littered with rocks and boulders.

The second-most attractive real estate in our solar system became uninhabitable.

"Is it realistic," McKay asks, "to rebuild that house from that pile of rubble?"

McKay believes it is. His approach, called *terraforming*, makes McKay something of a planetary Mr. Fix-it. Laying his blueprints on the table, McKay shows how we can reinflate the Martian atmosphere, turn up the air pressure, turn the heat back on, and get the water flowing again.

McKay believes we can restore Mars to a place

The surface of Mars is covered with rocks and boulders. Could life ever exist on this cold, dry planet? (NASA)

where life could prosper, as it was 3.8 billion years ago.

"Obviously," he says, "what you have to do first is warm up the planet. About twenty degrees centigrade warmer than it is now."

McKay would begin his warming with the release of *chlorofluorocarbons (CFCs)*, manmade greenhouse gases that were first produced in the 1930s. CFCs are used as coolants in air conditioners and refrigerators and as the propellants in hair sprays and shaving creams. On Earth, CFCs destroy our ozone layer and add to global warming.

But what is bad for life on Earth may be perfect for life on Mars. The Martian soil appears to be rich in chlorine, fluorine, carbon, hydrogen, and other chemicals needed to produce CFCs. McKay suggests setting down a nuclear-powered factory on Mars that would produce and release CFCs into the atmosphere. The factory would be run by astronauts.

As CFCs warmed the Martian atmosphere, carbon dioxide—trapped in the Martian soil and frozen in the polar caps—would escape into the air. This would contribute to the greenhouse effect.

As the temperature rose above freezing, water ice locked in the polar caps and Martian soil would become water vapor, another greenhouse gas. The warming would accelerate. The atmosphere would thicken. Air pressure would increase. Eventually, the water frozen in the Martian permafrost would begin to flow again.

Then McKay would let bugs take over.

"People are finding microorganisms," McKay says, "that can eat freon, which is a CFC. It's really fascinating stuff. Microorganisms seem to be able to eat just about anything. My thinking is," McKay adds, "that if there's a bug that can be trained to eat it, there's probably a bug that can be trained to make it. And so, what you would do is select bugs and then put them on Mars. They would make the freon constantly for you. Then you would not have to keep a factory on the surface, which would be expensive to maintain."

How long would this solution take?

The initial warming needed to support the hardiest bugs could occur in as little as 100 years. That is nothing, a blink of an eye in Mars's 4-billion-year existence. However, if the carbon dioxide is trapped deeper in the soil than present estimates, warming could take 100,000 years.

Turning Mars into a pleasant home for humans is

another story. People wandering around on a warmed Mars couldn't put down their breathing masks. The atmosphere would still lack oxygen. It took plants 3 billion years to fill Earth's air with enough oxygen for humans to be able to breathe. But that is not McKay's goal.

"A lot of people equate life with human life," McKay says. "But after many years of studying green algae and bacterial slime, I think it would be pretty amazing to have a planet with that kind of life on it."

McKay just wants Mars alive.

But what about Mars as the next frontier?

You are on your way to find out.

7
.

The Risks You Take

There is no turning back. You have been driven, like a tennis ball from a racket. You must land on Mars before you can be sent back home. Day after day, Earth becomes smaller and smaller. Your radioed voice takes longer to reach mission control. Halfway to Mars, you radio home, "Ma, how are you?"

It takes 20 minutes to hear your mother's answer.

The view outside your window stays the same day after day. You can see so many stars, they look like fog.

As gravity is pretty much meaningless to you now, so are the concepts of up and down. On Earth, "down" is the direction gravity pulls things. "Down" is where things fall. Well, nothing falls in your craft. Your clip-

Traveling to Mars means living without gravity for months on end.

board tied by a string to your wrist, you slowly drift in your cabin as you discuss the geology of Mars with another floating crewmate.

At this point, you do not talk about the risks. But you are an explorer. And like all great explorers, potentially deadly obstacles stalk your mission.

The first lurks within your own mind.

"All the conditions needed to drive a man to murder," the Russian cosmonaut Valery Ryumin wrote in his diary in 1980, "exist when you lock two people together in a small cabin in space for 2 months."

And what about six people in two small cabins for nearly three years? Your "habitat" is 15 feet in diameter and 16 feet tall. It has two decks, each with 8 feet of headroom. Will that be too confining? There are no screen doors opening onto porches and backyards. You are stuck. You will have no other people to confide in, to discuss your interests with, to listen to your jokes. You will be forced to listen to the same voices, day after day for three years. What will it be like listening to their worries, their stories, their jokes?

You will have your books on computer, movies and music to entertain and distract you, and your own small private space where you can be by yourself. There will be plenty of work for you to do to occupy your mind. But the questions remain. You are going to be with the same five people for almost three years. There will be arguments. There will be tension. How well will you manage the conflicts that arise? How well will you get along after spending months on the hostile, lonely surface of Mars? How close will you or your crewmates come to contemplating a violent crime?

Not too close. NASA spent years searching for the six best candidates. They knew what they were looking for, and you and your crewmates had it.

What was NASA looking for? Colonel Steve Nagel, an astronaut and space-shuttle commander, explains that the ideal explorer needs to be a team player.

"There's no room, on a trip to Mars, for a person who has to have his own way. You will need people who can get along under good, reasonable leadership. The crew will want their views heard, but when a decision is made they may not be in favor of, they will still salute and say, 'Yes, I'll do this.' "

That is you. Thousands of people applied to join the first Mars mission, but only you and your five crewmates were chosen. You passed the psychological testing, went through countless interviews, participated in role playing and crisis-intervention training. As a finalist, you were sent with a crew to train in Antarctica, the closest thing on Earth to Mars. You lived in a small habitat. Anytime you went out, you wore your space suit. You explored the terrain, looked for rocks and fossils. You took weather readings. You returned to your cabin and conducted experiments in your laboratory. You held meetings with your teammates. You worked out your differences. You helped keep everybody in high spirits. You performed beautifully.

Will the six of you continue to succeed as a team?

You have no choice.

Just for fun, you take out a postcard of your own, a diagram of our solar system with a tiny white arrow pointing to the black space between Earth and Mars.

"Here we are," the card says. "Enjoying the view!"

You write a note on the back to your family. When you hand-deliver it, you will be almost three years older.

You write that as you look at all those unblinking stars, you find it hard to believe there is not life

What would a postcard from Mars look like?

somewhere else in the universe. Why should life exist only on Earth? What makes Earth so special?

You cannot wait to get to Mars. Perhaps you will find some answers, something new to write home about.

You hope you are alive in three years to deliver your letters.

Weightless Dangers
and Invisible Bullets

You were not meant to live without gravity.

"The force of gravity has shaped the way our bodies are built," says Dr. Arnauld Nicogossian, chief medical officer for NASA. Just as fighting gravity on Earth made your bones, your heart, and your muscles strong, removing that gravity will make you weak.

On Earth, your heart pumped hard and blood vessels squeezed powerfully to pump your blood up against the downward pull of gravity. Now that you are weightless, your heart does not need to work as hard. It gets weaker. Your blood vessels slacken.

Along with your heart, the other muscles of your body weaken as well. Since they no longer have to push you up, keep you standing, or raise your weight, they lose their tone.

You exercise in your cabin to make your muscles work harder to prevent this decay. You ride your stationary bike. You walk on your treadmill. You think of the Russian cosmonaut Yuri Romanenko, who became something of a human hamster. Up in space for a year, he became so afraid of his body falling apart that he pedaled his stationary bike four hours a day, leaving him few hours to actually work.

You are not that afraid. You will be weightless for only six months at a time. When you land on Mars, where gravity is a little more than one third of Earth's, it will be easier to make your heart and muscles work hard again. You weighed 80 pounds back home. You will weigh 30 pounds on Mars.

What you cannot avoid is bone loss. Since your bones do not need to be as sturdy in space, they begin to shed the calcium that makes them strong. Most of this loss occurs in your spine and hips. The loss is not rapid, but if it is allowed to continue for over a year, your bones could become brittle and easily fracture.

What makes this bone loss doubly unpleasant is that calcium leaves your body through your kidneys. This could lead to kidney stones. Kidney stones are terribly painful.

There are other effects of living in weightlessness that are still not well understood. It is possible that your immune system, which helps you fight disease, also breaks down.

"As a matter of fact," Dr. Nicogossian explains, "space flight produces the symptoms of aging."

This was not a big deal for the astronauts who went into space before you. Most of those symptoms, with the exception of calcium loss, were reversible. All the astronaut had to do to get better was return to Earth.

But you will not be doing that for a long time.

"Can we protect astronauts one hundred percent against the risk of microgravity?" Dr. Nicogossia says. "The answer is no. There are no magic pills for gravity yet."

Still, you will not let gravity get you down. You have other bullets to dodge.

Galactic rays, which originate in the explosions of

stars, will constantly bombard your craft. Though you are not expected to receive high doses of this radiation, you cannot dismiss the possible dangers. Some scientists fear that the rays, which can penetrate anything, act like microscopic bullets. The damage they cause depends on what part of the body they strike and at what angle. Galactic rays could cause you or one of your crew members to experience loss of judgment, memory, and coordination.

More threatening are *solar flares,* which are intense bursts of radiation from the sun. Exposure to this radiation could cause anemia, infections, bleeding, and damage to your bone marrow. Long-term effects could lead to cancer.

Fortunately, solar flares are preceded by a warning: radio waves. Your crew could detect the flares an hour before they reach your ship. Given notice, you can retreat into a room in the craft that is insulated by your supply of food and water. This will protect you, and your food and water will not be damaged by the radiation from the flares.

The only problem would be if you are outside your

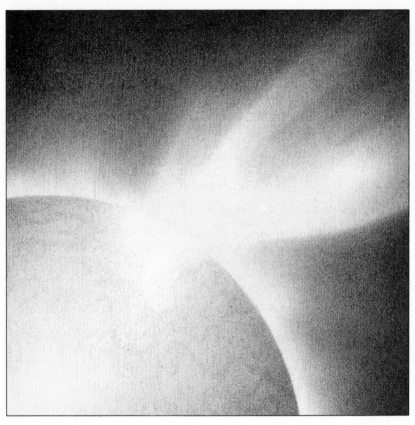

Solar flares, bursts of radiation from the sun, are among the dangers astronauts encounter in space.

craft, doing repair work, when the radio waves are detected. In that case, you might get hit by the flares before you made it back inside.

Then there are accidents, serious illness, and any

other medical emergency that might arise. One member of your crew might get sick enough in the next three years to require a hospital stay or surgery. That could be a problem.

"You can't build a flying hospital," Colonel Nagel says. "You can minimize the chances of something happening by physical screening." A physician can examine you and declare you healthy. But no physician can look into the future and declare you healthy for the next three years. Your crew can include a doctor. Your ship can carry certain medicines and equipment, but you cannot prepare for every possible emergency. As Colonel Nagel puts it, "You are going to have to assume some risk."

9

Packing Your Bags
and Paying Your Bills

You wonder if what you are doing is the right thing. The risks really do not bother you. You have faith in the scientists and engineers who put your program together. But you think of the cost of sending your crew to Mars: 50 billion dollars. What does that mean? How much is 50 billion dollars?

It is 200 dollars for every man, woman, and child in the United States. How many homes could be built with that money? How many medical bills could be paid? What rivers could be cleaned?

You doubt many other explorers cared about the money that was spent on their adventures. Sending you to Mars has employed tens of thousands of people.

It has brought Russia, much of Europe, and the United States together in the pursuit of a common goal. Millions of people pray for your success.

You open a snack of sandwich cookies. The average adult requires about 3 pounds of food, 5 pounds of water, and 2 pounds of oxygen a day. You can get by with a little less. For your long trip your crew of six will need to pack about 54,000 pounds of food, water, and oxygen. To save on space and weight, and to last a long time without spoiling, most of your food was *dehydrated*—its water removed. To prepare a meal, you just open a packet, add water, and put your rehydrated beef goulash into the microwave. In the next three years you will eat about 2,700 meals in this way.

You did not become an explorer for the food.

If you get bored, or hungry between meals, you can open a bag of peanuts or cookies.

"Sleeping is kind of weird," Colonel Nagel says. Your bed is actually a sleeping bag you climb into, then slip your arms through. "You zip it up, and you just kind of float there. It's very strange because you're not lying on anything. You're just floating." Your pillow

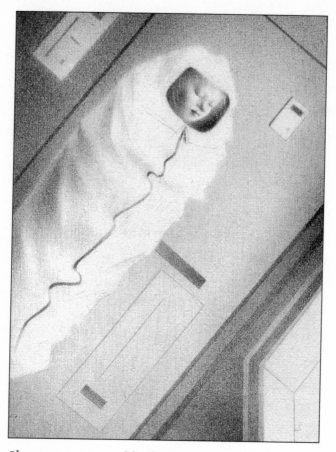

Sleeping in space is like floating in a pod.

is strapped to your head with a piece of Velcro.
Your toilet looks just like the one you have at home, only it works on a vacuum system, and it has a seat belt so you don't float away.

An artist's rendition of NASA's proposed Martian space station (Lockheed Martin)

You remind yourself you are a colonist, not a tourist. But unlike the Pilgrims, you will not be accommodated by a native civilization that has already mastered the art of living off the land. There will be nobody to greet you, and there will be no land to farm, streams to fish, or animals to hunt. Still, you cannot bring everything you will need with you.

Most significantly, you do not bring the rocket fuel for the return trip. Bringing that fuel would have made your ship impossibly heavy, too heavy to launch from Earth.

Two years before your lift-off, an unmanned rocket was sent to Mars, carrying a 40-ton payload. That cargo contained life-support systems, nearly a year's supply of food for your crew, the Earth Return Vehicle, and surface rovers. It also carried a robotic factory that instantly began sucking in the Martian air. This carbon dioxide was combined with hydrogen brought from Earth to make the methane rocket fuel needed for your return trip.

How convenient! A gas station awaits you on Mars! You think of the car trips you took on Earth. Next rest stop 50 million miles!

10

Life on Mars

You will look for evidence of life on Mars. You will look for fossils. You will have a rover, equipped with a pressurized cabin, to get you where you want to go. You will explore the dry rivers and lake beds. The hunting will not be easy. Fossils on Earth are tough to find, and the Earth has been teeming with life for billions of years. For an organism on Earth to become a fossil, it has to be buried shortly after it dies. Otherwise, other organisms will make a meal of it, and the wind and rain will sweep away its memory. If it is buried, it has to leave some hard clue. It could create an impression in soft mud. That sculpted mud could harden into rock. Or its bones can become

A scientist searches for fossils that would prove there was once life on Mars.

mineralized. Or it could be frozen. Or trapped in amber, or preserved in peat. Then it has to have been exposed to the surface only recently. If it showed up on the surface long ago, it would have been destroyed by the effects of wind and water.

Nobody is really sure how, if there was life on Mars, that life formed fossils. How hard then will your work be to find fossils on Mars?

"I live near Morrison, Colorado," says Robert Zubrin, a scientist and expert on Martian explorations. "It is one of the richest areas for finding dinosaur fossils in the world. I've never found one. Professional paleontologists come out here and it takes years before they make a serious find."

So, if you cannot find a dinosaur in Colorado, how easy will it be to find traces of life on Mars? If anything ever lived on Mars, most likely it was a lot smaller than an apatosaurus. It may not have had any hard parts to leave impressions in the Martian mud. Or its traces may have been erased by the geological forces of Mars, or by the effects of the ultraviolet radiation on the soil. You will be looking for the footprints of something that may never have walked, the remains of something that may never have lived.

But *you* will be proof that life can exist on Mars.

Soon after landing, your crew will cover your habitat with sandbags to protect it against ultraviolet radiation and solar flares. You will set up experimental greenhouses, to see what plants can be grown without soil, *hydroponically.* You will determine what needs to be done to the Martian soil so that it can support plant life. Perhaps you will set up pools for fish, as a future source of protein. You will study the Martian weather and geology. You will investigate the possibilities of terraforming.

In your rovers, you will hunt for areas where you could dig for frozen water. You will begin preparing Mars for the next crew to follow you in two years.

View from the Viking 2's *lander of the barren landscape of Mars*

Already, another unmanned payload is on its way, sent up two weeks after your launch. Along with your pioneering work, this unmanned moving van will help prepare Mars for the people who follow you. They in turn will prepare the planet for the next group of colonists.

Slowly, a string of frontier towns will arise on the pink Martian surface. Perhaps new laws will be written to govern these settlers, new governments established. With Earth over 35 million miles away, with the spoken word taking nearly 20 minutes to reach Earth, and a response taking another 20 minutes, the New Martians will grow more independent of their mother planet.

One day, a baby will be born on Mars, the first Martian. If the human body grows strong in order to fight against gravity on Earth, how will that child's body develop on Mars? What if that child's heart muscles and bones grow only strong enough to survive the weak gravity of Mars? Will that first Martian ever be able to visit the Earth?

Imagine an adult female Martian who wishes to visit the green, oxygen-rich planet of her parents. She wishes to see trees, oceans, dolphins, and blue skies. She weighs 45 Martian pounds, roughly the same as 110 Earth pounds.

She will travel six months through the zero gravity of space weighing next to nothing. Slowly her heart, muscles, and skeleton will grow weaker. Then, on landing on the Earth, she will suddenly weigh 110 pounds.

Will her heart survive?

Your ship travels silently through space. Are you an explorer, or are you simply a seed, carried across great distances to land on new, strange soil?

Why are you going?

How will you change the history of life on Mars?

Update

On January 14, 2004, eight years after this book was first published, President George W. Bush announced that he would like NASA to begin planning for the human exploration of the moon as a first step toward the exploration of Mars.

"Inspired by all that has come before and guided by clear objectives, today we set a new course for America's space program," the president said. "We will give NASA a new focus and vision for future exploration. We will build new ships to carry man forward into the universe, to gain a new foothold on the moon, and to prepare for the new journeys to the worlds beyond our own."

The president chose to give his speech on the anniversary of two historic moments in exploration, while a third historic occurrence was taking place millions of miles away. Nearly a year earlier, on February 1, 2003, seven astronauts had been killed as their space shuttle *Columbia* exploded just before its scheduled landing. Upon launch of the ship, a piece of foam had flown off a fuel tank and struck the shuttle, damaging the heat protection tiles on its left wing. At the time, NASA engineers did not consider the damage serious. However, when the shuttle re-entered the Earth's atmosphere at 15,000 miles per hour, the intense heat that surrounded the craft entered the wound in the damaged wing. The shuttle ignited and exploded in its descent, scattering debris and human remains over hundreds of miles across East Texas. The tragedy reminded all of the very dangerous risks astronauts take as they explore space.

The second historic moment in exploration was the 200th anniversary of the Lewis and Clark expedition to explore the new lands acquired in the Louisiana Purchase. President Bush cited this event as a model for future explorations. "They made that journey in the spirit of discovery, to learn the potential of the vast new territory and to chart the way for others to follow." While remembering the shuttle astronauts, President Bush also urged his listeners to recall the early age of exploration and westward expansion that allowed the United States to become a great nation.

While the president spoke of America's westward expansion, another historic event, which could be thought of as a robotic version of Lewis and Clark, was occurring about 35 million miles away on the planet Mars. On January 4, 2004, NASA had landed the robot explorer *Spirit* in Gusev Crater, just south of the Martian equator. This landing would be followed 21 days later by the landing of another robot explorer, *Opportunity*, on a smooth plain near the Martian equator and halfway around the planet from *Spirit*. The mission for both robots, which cost over $800 million, would be to look for any evidence that water had once flowed on the now dry and dusty planet.

President Bush stood at this crossroads in history to look into the future and challenge NASA to think big.

He asked NASA to begin the planning necessary to land humans on the moon by 2015.

"With the experience and knowledge gained on the moon," President Bush challenged NASA, "we will then be ready to take the next steps of space exploration, human missions to Mars and to the worlds beyond."

"I'll believe it when I see it," says Nadine Barlow, one of the scientists who worked on the planning for the robot explorer *Spirit*. "It's a nice idea, but the big problem is money. President Bush has pledged a billion dollars, and that is simply not enough to get humans to Mars." After all, Barlow points out, that is only slightly more than the cost of the current mission to land two robots.

Barlow does believe, however, that sending humans to the moon first is a good idea. "The astronauts can do a practice run for Mars. They can build colonies. They can use the moon as a test base for exploring." Barlow believes training on the hostile surface of the moon could teach us valuable lessons about how to survive on Mars.

Launching a ship to Mars from the moon may not offer any advantage to launching it from Earth, but the president's thinking is understandable. The gravitational pull on the surface of the moon is about one sixth that of Earth's and this would make it easier for a rocket ship to blast off into space. The rocket would also need less fuel for liftoff. This would allow it to carry more of the scientific instruments and machinery necessary for the astronauts' missions and survival on Mars. There are some problems, however. The instruments and the machinery needed for those Mars missions would probably be built on Earth. What would be the advantage of leaving from the moon if most of your supplies had to be blasted off from Earth first?

Barlow's second concern is people. A NASA space launch involves hundreds, if not thousands of people. How many of them would need to be on the moon to make sure a launch to Mars was successful? How would they be sustained? How would we house them, feed them, provide enough water for them, and make sure they had the equipment necessary to carry out their mission? How expensive would it be to sustain a large colony on the moon? If launching two robots to Mars costs over $800 million, how much will it take to send hundreds of people to the moon and keep them alive and working in an airless and completely dry environment?

That said, many scientists love the idea of going to Mars. They believe completely in President Bush's dream. And while many of them would like to be among the first to explore the red planet, they will have to do their current exploring through the eyes of robots.

Scientists such as Barlow could not be happier. Barlow looks at the search for water on Mars as an opportunity to travel billions of years back in time to when the Earth and Mars were new planets and quite possibly resembled each other in their geology and atmosphere. At that time, when pieces of unformed planets were still smashing the Earth and Mars, creating huge craters, Barlow believes that both Mars and Earth had flowing water. Yet as these planetary siblings developed, they came to resemble each other less and less. Earth, the larger of the two, was gifted with a greater gravitational force, which allowed it to keep its atmosphere from drifting off into space. Earth's tectonic plates kept moving, allowing for earthquakes and volcanoes to reshape the planet and release carbon dioxide into the atmosphere. The water on Earth allowed the chemistry of life to develop. That early life began producing oxygen, which in turn allowed for animal life to flourish.

Mars, the runt, farther from the sun and colder, with no tectonic action, became a cold, bone-dry desert. As its larger sibling developed and flourished, Mars dried up.

What happened to its water? When did it stop flowing? Could it be frozen beneath the crust of Mars?

As this is written, the European probe *Observer* is orbiting Mars, using ground-penetrating radar to look deep under the Martian crust to see if there are hidden bodies of frozen water.

The robots *Spirit* and *Observer,* six-wheeled geology labs, are cruising around the equatorial regions of the planet, examining minerals and looking to see if any of them developed in the presence of flowing water.

Gusev Crater appears to be a dried-out lake bed. There seems to be a dry riverbed flowing into it from the south and exiting from the north. Could there be remains of water-created minerals in this basin?

The *Meridiani Planum,* a flat plain, is littered with a mineral called gray hematite. On Earth, gray hematite is usually formed in the presence of flowing water, although sometimes it can be created through the activity of volcanic lava.

What will these robots discover? What new missions will be launched? How will future expeditions prepare the rocky, red, cold desert planet of Mars for the water-loving, oxygen-breathing explorers from Earth?

These are questions you will be able to answer over these next few years.

Are you getting ready to go?

Bibliography

Allegre, Claude, and Stephen Schneider. "The Evolution of the Earth." *Scientific American,* October 1994.

Baker, David, and Robert Zubrin. "Humans to Mars, 1999." *Aerospace America,* August 1990.

Begley, Sharon. "Next Stop, Mars." *Newsweek,* 25 July 1994.

Berliner, Don. *Living In Space* (Minneapolis: Lerner Publications, 1993).

Broad, William. "Drillers Find Lost World of Ancient Microbes." *New York Times,* 4 October 1994.

Camerole, Peter. *The Story of the Red Planet* (London: Chapman & Hall, 1992).

Cantril, Hadley. *The Invasion from Mars* (Princeton: Princeton University Press, 1966).

Carrol, Michael. "Digging Deeper for Life on Mars." *Astronomy,* April 1988.

Chaisson, Eric. *Cosmic Dawn* (New York: W. W. Norton, 1981).

Collins, Michael. "Mission to Mars." *National Geographic,* November 1988.

DeCampli, William. "The Limits of Manned Space Flight." *The Sciences,* September 1986.

Diamond, Neil. "Interview with Story Musgrave." *Omni,* August 1994.

Friedman, Louis. "Return to the Martian Surface." *Ad Astra,* September–October 1992.

Gannon, Robert. "The Unbearable Lightness of Space Travel." *Popular Science,* March 1992.

Joels, Kerry Mark. *The Space Shuttle Operator's Manual* (New York: Ballantine Books, 1982).

Kieffer, Hugh, ed. *MARS* (Tucson: University of Arizona Press, 1992).

Kluger, Jeffrey. "Mars: In Earth's Image." *Discover,* September 1992.

McDonough, Thomas. *SPACE: The Next Twenty-Five Years* (New York: John Wiley & Sons, Inc., 1989).

McKay, Chris. "What Should Be the Next U.S. Mission to Mars?" *Mars Underground News V,* Summer 1993.

McKay, Chris, and Robert Zubrin. "Mars Needs Humans." *Ad Astra,* September–October 1992.

Mitton, Jacqueline. "Rendezvous with the Red Planet." *New Scientist,* 3 April 1993.

Moore, Patrick. *Guide to Mars* (New York: W. W. Norton and Company, 1977).

Mundell, Ian. "Stop the Rocket I Want to Get Off." *New Scientist,* April 1993.

Murray, Bruce C. *Journey Into Space* (New York: W. W. Norton and Company, 1989).

Nadis, Steve. "Mars, the Final Frontier." *New Scientist,* February 1994.

Raab, Carl. "Global Warming, Understanding the Forecast" (working draft, American Museum of Natural History, New York, 1992).

Rabiotti, Aldo. "Spacelab the Physiological Challenges." *Astronomy,* March 1985.

Reynolds, Glen. "'What About the Environmental Impact Statement?': The Law and Ethics of Terraforming." *Ad Astra,* September–October 1992.

Ronan, Colin, ed. *Science Explained* (New York: Henry Holt, 1983).

Sagan, Carl. *Cosmos* (New York: Random House, 1980).

———. "The Search for Extraterrestrial Life." *Scientific American,* October 1994.

Stoker, C., and S. Welch, eds. "The Case for Mars." Jet Propulsion Laboratory Publication 86-28.

Svarney, Patricia Barnes. "The Once and Future Planet." *Ad Astra,* September–October 1992.

Trefil, James. *1001 Things Everyone Should Know About Science* (New York: Doubleday, 1992).

Zubrin, Robert. "The Terraforming Debate." *Mars Underground News V,* Summer 1993.

Index

(Page numbers in *italic* refer to illustrations.)

Other Books by David Getz
and Peter McCarty

FROZEN GIRL

"A gripping, detailed text and scattered
black-and-white photographs and illustrations tell
of the discovery of a five-hundred-year-old mummy
in the Andes Mountains."
—*The Horn Book Guide*

FROZEN MAN

"Young readers should find this book fascinating,
as Getz describes the discovery, recovery (barely!),
and scientific study of this man who died
approximately 5,000 years ago."
—*School Library Journal*

PURPLE DEATH

"An intriguing look at the human side
of the mysterious disease that in the fall of 1918
killed more than half a million people around the world,
most of the healthy young men."
—*VOYA*